THE PROMISE: extreme for Jesus

Are you ready for the truth? Can you <u>handle</u> the truth? Well, this is it… God has a plan for your life and He's made promises <u>galore</u> for your future! When you make the choice to be **extreme for Jesus**, you set the stage for *real change* and *great adventure* in the days ahead.

During this awesome series, you'll hear the *bold truth* from well-known youth leader Ron Luce. With a life committed to God and a heart on fire for teens, he helps open the door to God's extreme promises about:

- ❖ HOPE
- ❖ YOUR LIFESTYLE
- ❖ YOUR RELATIONSHIPS
- ❖ MAKING A DIFFERENCE

These powerful sessions present the straight truth in a way that sticks with you! You'll get some hard-hitting scriptural advice and learn some life-changing biblical principles. Even when troubles strike, you can be prepared to overcome them.

The Promise: extreme for Jesus is an uncompromising study for a new generation of believers who refuse to sit still, but would rather *stand strong* for God!

Ron Luce is the president and founder of *Teen Mania Ministries* and the host of a popular weekly teen television program called *Acquire the Fire*. He travels the country and the world proclaiming the gospel of Jesus Christ and working to fulfill his mission to teens.

His vision is to empower today's young people to be extreme for Jesus by encouraging them to make a <u>real</u> difference in their schools, their communities, and their world!

"Yours' is a generation of destiny… seize it!"

THE PROMISE
extreme for Jesus

by

RON LUCE

Companion Study Materials:

Extreme Teen Bible
Extreme for Jesus Promise Book

All Scriptures used in this participant's guide, unless otherwise noted, are taken from the New King James Version. Copyright 1982 by Thomas Nelson, Inc. Used by permission. All rights reserved.

HOW THE SESSIONS ARE DESIGNED

- ☑ Each session has an introductory page with three categories: *Gimme Some Truth*, *The Inside Line*, and *Extreme Promises*. This page is designed to help you prepare for the lesson.

- ☑ Each Bible study time consists of a *Video Discussion* featuring comments by Ron Luce.

- ☑ *TALK about a Revolution!* is a page of discussion questions that will allow you to talk about concepts and principles from the lesson. It will also provide a foundation for personal reflection and real-life application.

HOW TO GET THE MOST OUT OF THIS VIDEO SERIES

Before the group meets… Preview the Session
- ☑ Look through the lesson in your participant's guide.
- ☑ Review the topics that will be discussed.
- ☑ Check out the Scripture passages that will be studied.
- ☑ Take notice of the specific questions that will be explored.
- ☑ Pray for God to prepare your heart for what He wants you to learn.

When the group meets… Participate in the Session
- ☑ Take notes throughout the session, filling in the answers to questions provided during the video lesson.
- ☑ Follow along with the Scripture passages.
- ☑ Share your thoughts during the discussion.
- ☑ Ask and answer questions.

After the group meets… Review the Session
- ☑ Look through the lesson in your participant's guide.
- ☑ Review your notes and answers.
- ☑ Study the Scripture passages further and commit one of the featured verses to memory.

ABOUT THE AUTHOR

Ron Luce is the president and founder of *Teen Mania Ministries*. He started this successful youth-oriented organization with his wife, Katie, in 1986. *Teen Mania* is all about helping young people be extreme for God and encompasses, but is not limited to, the following:

Teen Mania Global Expeditions
Acquire the Fire Youth Conventions and Dome Events
Acquirethefire.com
Teen Mania Honor Academy

Ron also hosts a weekly television program, **Acquire the Fire**, which airs on several broadcast outlets. He has traveled to more than 50 countries, proclaiming the gospel of Jesus Christ. His dream is to empower young people to take a stand for Christ in their schools and in the world.

Table of Contents

Session 1
    Extreme Promises of Hope   1

Session 2
    Extreme Promises about Your Lifestyle   10

Session 3
    Extreme Promises for Your Personal Relationships   18

Session 4
    Extreme Promises about Making a Difference   27

THE PROMISE
extreme for Jesus

Session 1
HOPE

Extreme Promises of Hope

GIMME SOME TRUTH:

> For You are my hope, O Lord GOD;
> *You are* my trust from my youth.
> (Psalm 71:5)

> Let us hold fast the confession of *our* hope without wavering,
> for He who promised *is* faithful.
> (Hebrews 10:23)

Hope is necessary to our daily lives because it helps us focus on our future. It gives us the desire to press on. The source of hope is the Lord Himself because He is the loving designer of our eternal future. Rest assured that God can be trusted to keep His promises.

THE INSIDE LINE:

> He loves each one of us, as if there were only
> one of us.
> (St. Augustine)

EXTREME PROMISES:
(The following Bible verses will introduce you to some of the life-changing concepts in this session.)

When you are depressed
Psalm 147:3
1 Peter 4:12-13

When you are guilty
Psalm 32:5
1 John 1:9

When you are worried
Isaiah 26:3-4
John 14:27

Video Discussion

Where can you go to find and fortify your hope everyday?
_____
_____

*(Check out **Romans 15:4** for the answer.)*

FOCUS ON A FIRM FOUNDATION

B_____ y_____ l_____ on the Word of God.

Come to a place where you _____ God's Word.

Read the i_____ m_____ for your life.

The World vs. The Word

Name three ways in which people are constantly fed the world's message?

T_____   M_____   M_____

How did the Lord make a difference in Brendon's life?
_____
_____
_____

What happened for Stephanie when she decided to "try Jesus?"
_____
_____
_____

Video Discussion

Have you ever been in a situation of hopelessness?
_____

If so, what was the worst thing about being in that place?
_____
_____

What should you do when the situation appears hopeless?
_____
_____

*(Check out **2 Kings 19:14-19** for the answer.)*

ATTENTION
Extreme Truth Ahead…

GOD IS ON YOUR SIDE!!

Name two young people in the Bible who experienced the intervention and faithfulness of God in their lives?

  1) J_____
  2) D_____

*(Want to know more about these radical Christians? Read their cutting edge profiles in your **Extreme Teen Bible** or check out **Genesis 37-50** & **1 Samuel 16-1 Kings 2**.)*

IF GOD IS _____ _____, WHO CAN BE AGAINST US?

Video Discussion

When you have a _____ with Jesus… when He is _____ to you… that's what gives you hope!

According to Ron, what are three actions that you can take every day to build your relationship with Jesus?

1) Have a _____ _____
2) _____ the _____
3) Practice _____ _____

What to do…
WHEN YOU ARE DEPRESSED

Why was David discouraged and depressed?
_____
_____

Did David have a valid reason to be discouraged?
_____
_____

In the middle of being totally discouraged, what was David's response?
_____
_____
_____

PSALM 42:5

Why are you cast down,
O my soul?
And *why* are you disquieted
within me?
Hope in God, for I shall
yet praise Him
For the help of His
countenance.

Video Discussion

What to do…
WHEN YOU ARE GUILTY

Don't allow feelings of frustration and anger at yourself to push you away from God. It's better to come back with _____ than to live outside of God's presence.

According to Revelation 12:10, Satan is "the _____ of our _____." This means that he is pointing the finger at you. He wants to make you feel so bad that you won't ask for forgiveness.

What instructions does the Bible give us for dealing with guilt?
_____
_____
_____

1 JOHN 1:9

If we confess our sins,

He is faithful and just

to forgive us *our* sins

and to cleanse us from all

unrighteousness.

ATTENTION
Extreme Truth Ahead…

NOTHING CAN SEPARATE YOU FROM GOD'S LOVE!!

Video Discussion

What should you do the next time you really blow it?

    1) C_____ your sin
    2) R_____
    3) Be t_____
    4) Get into the W_____ of _____

What to do…
WHEN YOU ARE WORRIED

What is the danger of falling into the habit of worrying?

_____
_____
_____

According to Matthew 6:31-34, what does Jesus say about worry?

_____
_____
_____

As a Christian, you have the freedom to **choose** what you will dwell on. What should your first step be in laying down your worries before God?

_____
_____

ROMANS 8:38-39

For I am persuaded that
neither death nor life,
nor angels nor principalities
nor powers, nor things present
nor things to come, nor height
nor depth, nor any other
created thing, shall be able
to separate us from the love
of God which is in
Christ Jesus our Lord.

TALK about a Revolution!

Why is it necessary that we have hope in our daily lives?
_____
_____
_____

You heard Brendon and Stephanie express how their lives changed when they turned to the Lord in their hopelessness. How has the Lord made a difference in your life?
_____
_____
_____

According to God's Word, how should you handle depression?
_____
_____
_____

Read Psalm 103:11-12. What does the Lord do with the guilt and transgressions of those who belong to Him?
_____
_____
_____

How can you combat worry? *(Take a look at **Exodus 14:13** & **Philippians 4:6**.)*
_____
_____
_____

Why should you trust God as your source of hope? *(Search your Bible for the attributes & characteristics of God. You can start with **Hebrews 6:18-19, 10:23** & **1 Peter 1:21**.)*
_____
_____
_____

HOPE Notes

THE PROMISE
extreme for Jesus

Session 2
LIFESTYLE

Extreme Promises about Your Lifestyle

GIMME SOME TRUTH:

Get wisdom! Get understanding!
Do not forget, nor turn away from the
words of my mouth.
(Proverbs 4:5)

Show me Your ways, O LORD;
Teach me Your paths.
Lead me in Your truth and teach me,
For You *are* the God of my salvation;
On You I wait all the day.
(Psalm 25:4-5)

"God is looking for young people whose hearts are so committed to Him that they want to obey Him in every way. He is looking for young people who will follow Him, even when they don't quite understand the reason for His command or instruction."
--*Ron Luce*

THE INSIDE LINE:

Whoever falls from God's right hand
is caught into his left.
(Edwin Markham)

…I will not forget you.
See, I have inscribed you on the palms
Of My Hands…
(Isaiah 49:15-16)

EXTREME PROMISES:
(The following Bible verses will introduce you to some of the life-changing concepts in this session.)

    Isaiah 48:17-18 1 Corinthians 6:20
    Romans 13:13-14 Colossians 3:12-17

Video Discussion

If you live by God's Word, His _____ will _____ you!

What is the real truth about God's commandments? How can they affect your life?
_____
_____
_____

What happened when Wes took the advice of his youth minister to "grow up, be a man and seek God's help?"
_____
_____
_____

ATTENTION
Extreme Truth Ahead…

⬇

OBEY GOD… AND HIS PROMISES WILL BLOW YOU AWAY!!

Obedience to God is essential to your relationship with Him. It is an act of faith that puts into motion God's saving work in your life. Make the choice to live within His protecting parameters every day, even if you don't always understand.

Video Discussion

What does the world want you to believe about having pre-marital sex, doing drugs and drinking alcohol?
_____
_____
_____

GOD COMMANDS US TO L_____ A P_____ LIFE.

He promises that if you do this, you're going to have:
    a blessed f_____
    a blessed h_____
    an understanding of the s_____ of _____,
    _____ and sexual intimacy

What happens when you allow an outside chemical to alter your brain?
_____
_____
_____
_____

Sometimes you _____ the guidelines of God and sometimes you _____.

What is God looking for from His children?
_____
_____
_____
_____

Video Discussion

1 CORINTHIANS 6:19-20

Or do you not know
that your body is the temple
of the Holy Spirit *who* is in
you, whom you have from God,
and you are not your own?
For you were bought at
a price; therefore glorify
God in your body and
in your spirit, which are God's.

Why does a wise person decide to follow the rules?
_____
_____
_____

Remember that you may be forgiven, but there are still _____ to your actions.

How should you relate to others who may not understand your life of obedience?
_____
_____
_____

There is a _____ of honor by which God wants us to live. What accompanies this?
_____

Define a life of "honor."
_____
_____

Video Discussion

ATTENTION
Extreme Truth Ahead…

IN CHRIST, YOU ARE FREE!!

Before you start dealing with the rules, God wants to change your h_____. Then your l_____ will change. He cares about you and is committed to helping you. So commit yourself to him every day and watch what He will do!

Have you ever made any lifestyle choices that you later regretted? If so, what were the consequences you experienced?
_____
_____
_____

Now is the time to determine in your heart to make the right choices. Don't live with regrets! Do things God's way and begin right now!

DEUTERONOMY 28:1-2

Now it shall come to pass, if you diligently obey the voice of the LORD your God, to observe carefully all His commandments which I command you today, that the LORD your God will set you high above all nations of the earth. And all these blessings shall come upon you and overtake you, because you obey the voice of the LORD your God…

TALK about a Revolution!

How can you know that you are making good lifestyle choices over bad ones?

_____
_____
_____

*(Check out **Proverbs 1:7**, **Matthew 16:26** & **Galatians 5:22-23** for some ideas.)*

What specific guidelines does God set forth in the Bible to help you have an incredible sex life when you're married?

_____
_____
_____

*(Take a look at **1 Thessalonians 4:4-5** & **Hebrews 13:4**.)*

Why do you think that young people turn to drugs and alcohol in their lives?

_____
_____

How should Christians respond to offers of drugs and alcohol?

_____
_____

Think about this next question and be honest with yourself. What kind of life do you really want to live?

_____
_____
_____

What are the rewards of living a Godly lifestyle?

_____
_____

LIFESTYLE Notes

THE PROMISE
extreme for Jesus

Session 3
RELATIONSHIPS

Extreme Promises for Your Relationships

GIMME SOME TRUTH:

...I have called you friends,
for all things that I heard from My Father
I have made known to you.
(John 15:15b)

But I say to you who hear: Love your enemies,
do good to those who hate you,
bless those who curse you,
and pray for those who spitefully use you.
(Luke 6:27-28)

Many people today have a lot of acquaintances but few deep relationships or true friendships. Godly relationships are very important because they provide value, depth and support throughout life. The Bible offers wonderful instruction on how to deal with all types of relationships. Dig in and find out!

THE INSIDE LINE:

A heart stitched with prayer is more precious
to God than a tapestry of gold.
(Anonymous)

One of the best ways to care about other people
is to <u>really</u> pray for them.
(Ron Luce)

EXTREME PROMISES:
(The following Bible verses will introduce you to some of the life-changing concepts in this session.)

Deuteronomy 15:7-8	Romans 12:3	1 Peter 3:9-10
Psalm 68:5	James 5:16	1 John 3:16-18

Video Discussion

According to scripture, what is the mark of true friendship? How does Jesus characterize His friends?
_____
_____
_____

*(Review **John 15:13-15** for some guidance.)*

Be careful not to take [God's] friendship for granted. He isn't like your friends at school, just as imperfect as you are. He is God. While you're learning to love Him as your best friend, don't ever lose sight of how awesome He is and of all the incredible gifts He gives you. Start to think of yourself as a friend of Jesus.

--Extreme Teen Bible

Extreme Reminder!

God has promises for <u>every</u> part of your life.
As you apply His Word, then your life gets
be_____ and bl_____.

What specific relationships are important to you?
_____
_____
_____

What did Natalia have to learn about forgiveness in order to restore a relationship with her father?
_____
_____
_____

Video Discussion

EPHESIANS 6:1-3

Children, obey your parents
in the LORD, for this is right.
"Honor your father and mother,"
which is the first
commandment with promise:
*"that it may be well with you
and you may live long
on the earth."*

How should you handle conflict with your parents?
_____
_____
_____
_____

ATTENTION
Extreme Truth Ahead...

GOD THINKS YOU ARE AWESOME!!

The bottom line is this…   Even if you may disagree with your parents on some things, you should honor them because of the God-given _____ they hold.

God is the Master Designer and this is His design: Obedience leads to right choices and a good life, but rebellion leads to regret.   --Extreme Teen Bible

Video Discussion

What <u>specific</u> promise does the Lord attach to the command of honoring your parents?

_____

_____

PROVERBS 13:20

He who walks with

wise *men* will be wise,

But the companion of fools

will be destroyed.

How should you handle negative peer pressure?

_____

_____

_____

Have you ever had to deal with bad peer pressure? If so, how did you respond to your specific situation?

_____

_____

ATTENTION
Extreme Truth Ahead…

HANG OUT WITH WISE PEOPLE AND YOU WILL GAIN WISDOM!!

Video Discussion

Try not to use the "limited options" argument as an excuse for not having Christian friends. If your school doesn't have much to offer, then explore local youth groups, consult your parents for help, or check out Christian websites for leads.

You have to be _____ for the right kind of friends. You must have a passion to seek out Godly peers.

TAKE THE LEAD
If your church youth group has become passive and mediocre, don't settle for it. You can be the leader in becoming radical for Christ. Dare to be bold in your love for Jesus. Who knows? It may just spread like wildfire!

EPHESIANS 4:32

And be kind to one another, tenderhearted, forgiving one another, even as God in Christ forgave you.

Have you ever been in a position of needing to forgive someone who has hurt you? If so, were you able to offer that forgiveness?
_____
_____
_____

How should you handle someone who seems not to deserve forgiveness?
_____
_____
_____

Video Discussion

How does the inability to forgive manifest itself in a person?
_____
_____
_____
_____

KEYS TO FORGIVENESS

You won't always <u>feel</u> like forgiving.
Choose to forgive <u>in</u> <u>advance</u>.
When you <u>choose</u> to forgive, it does you good.
<u>God</u> <u>forgave</u> <u>you</u>, so you must forgive others.

ATTENTION
Extreme Truth Ahead…

IF YOU WANT GRACE… YOU NEED TO GIVE GRACE!!

Lord, I need to confess that I have not forgiven, as I should. I lay this burden down and at this moment I choose to forgive. I am making this decision right now, even though I may not feel like it. I ask for your restoration in this area of my life and look to you for Godly relationships. In Jesus' name. Amen.

TALK about a Revolution!

What can you do if you are having trouble making good friends?

_____

_____

*(See **Hebrews 13:5** & **Proverbs 17:17**. Take another look at **Ephesians 4:32**.)*

How should you respond to your mother and father, even if you disagree with them?

_____

_____

How can you tell the difference between good and bad peer pressure?

_____

_____

_____

How can you prepare in advance to deal with unwanted peer pressure?

_____

_____

According to 1 Peter 3:8-9, what specific response should you have to someone who has hurt you?

_____

_____

Why should you choose forgiveness instead of anger and resentment?

_____

_____

*(Read **Mark 11:25** & the parable of the unforgiving servant in **Matthew 18:21-35**.)*

RELATIONSHIP Notes

THE PROMISE
extreme for Jesus

Session 4
MAKING A DIFFERENCE

Extreme Promises about Making a Difference

GIMME SOME TRUTH:

Let no one despise your youth, but be an
example to the believers in word, in conduct,
in love, in spirit, in faith, in purity.
(1 Timothy 4:12)

I can do all things through Christ
who strengthens me.
(Philippians 4:13)

The Bible is filled with examples of young people who **stepped out** to be used by God. They had never been to seminary, nor did they have degrees. Still, they made a difference. It was their simple obedience to God and their **no excuses** attitude that opened the door to God's plan. He wants to use you, too! The Lord is counting on you to stand up and make a difference while you are young.

THE INSIDE LINE:

Yours' is a generation of destiny...
seize it!
(G. Robertson)

EXTREME PROMISES:
(The following Bible verses will introduce you to some of the life-changing concepts in this session.)

Exodus 4:2-5	Matthew 5:14-16	1 Peter 1:22
Daniel 1:17	Matthew 28:19-20	1 Peter 4:11

Video Discussion

Extreme Reminder!

God wants to use _____ of us to make a difference in this world!

You are here on this earth for a _____. There are people in this world that only you can touch.

How does your age affect God's ability to use you?
_____
_____
_____

Name at least three young people in the Bible that God used mightily.
_____
_____

(Want to know more about these radical young Christians? Read some of their cutting edge profiles in your **Extreme Teen Bible** or check out **2 Kings 22:1 - 23:30, Daniel 2:46 – 3:30 & Luke 1:26 – 2:52**.)

**God doesn't measure your maturity
by how old you are.
He measures your maturity
by how much you
obey His Word.**

Video Discussion

What part should you play in preparing yourself to be used by God?
_____
_____
_____

What change did Jay make that allowed the Lord to step in and really bless his gifts?
_____
_____
_____

What did Donny's experience teach him about his ability to make a difference in the world?
_____
_____
_____

ATTENTION
Extreme Truth Ahead…

YOU CAN MAKE A DIFFERENCE AND YOU CAN START RIGHT NOW!!

Video Discussion

JAMES 1:19

So then,
my beloved brethren,
let every man be
swift to hear,
slow to speak,
slow to wrath…

Even if you're not a public speaker, you can still make a difference. How can you get started?
_____
_____
_____

What should you do if you've messed up, but still want to be used by God?
_____
_____
_____

The World's View   vs.   **The Word's View**
We should live to make   We should live to make
a _____ .   a _____ .

ATTENTION
Extreme Truth Ahead…

GOD PUT **YOU** HERE TO MAKE A DIFFERENCE**!!**

Video Discussion

List four specific actions that will open the door to make a difference in someone else's life.

    To L_____
    To L_____
    To Show R_____
    To S_____

God is not looking for **excuses**. If you have a heart to serve Him, He's going to speak to you about your gifts. Remember Jeremiah!

JEREMIAH 1:6-8

Then said I:
"Ah, Lord GOD!
Behold, I cannot speak,
for I *am* a youth."
But the LORD said to me:
"Do not say, 'I *am* a youth,'
For you shall go to all
to whom I send you,
And whatever I
command you,
you shall speak.
Do not be afraid of their faces,
For I *am* with you
to deliver you," says the LORD.

The promises of Jeremiah are for <u>you</u>, as well!

What should you do if the world comes against your dream to make a difference for Jesus?

_____
_____

Video Discussion

The wonderful truth about God is that He can take any gift you possess, no matter what it is, and find a way to use it for His glory. Take some time to seek the Lord about your gifts. Ask Him to speak to you and show you how to use the talents He's given you. Then, find ways to develop those gifts.

Listen to the words of Jesus…

LUKE 10:2-3

Then He said to them,
"The harvest truly *is* great,
but the laborers *are* few;
therefore pray the Lord
of the harvest to send out
laborers into His harvest,
Go your way; behold,
I send you out as
lambs among wolves…"

Go out into the world **without fear** and make your life count while you are young. Stay in the Word and seek the Lord… and watch what God will do!

ATTENTION
Extreme Truth Ahead…

YOU CAN SPARK A REVOLUTION!!

TALK about a Revolution!

Fill in the blank. *The only people God has to work with are _____ people.*

Take a moment to list your gifts and talents. (Think outside the box!) :)
_____
_____
_____
_____

Make a commitment to seek God about your gifts. Make yourself available to Him and ask Him to speak to you about how you can make a difference. When the Lord begins to instruct you… write it down.
_____
_____
_____
_____

Write down two people in your circle of acquaintances who need God's love.
1) _____ 2) _____
Make a promise to reach out to them in a <u>real</u> way. Pray for them and think about how you can give them encouragement.

What are you showing when you give your full attention to others?
_____
_____
_____

MAKING A DIFFERENCE
Notes

> **Here are a few radical suggestions for letting your faith in Christ make an *extreme* difference:**

- ➤ Participate in your school's *See you at the Pole* event

- ➤ Organize a prayer group at your campus

- ➤ Get involved at church – don't just take up a chair

- ➤ Dig into a Bible study or accountability group

- ➤ Raise your own support and go on a missions trip

- ➤ Read a Christian book – or your Bible – during study hall

- ➤ Wear a shirt with a Christian message as a conversation piece

1 Peter 3:15-16

But sanctify the Lord God in your hearts, and always *be* ready to *give* a defense to everyone who asks you a reason for the hope that is in you, with meekness and fear; having a good conscience, that when they defame you as evildoers, those who revile your good conduct in Christ may be ashamed.

37